painting glass

WITH THE COLOR SHAPER   PAULA DESIMONE

GLOUCESTER MASSACHUSETTS

QUARRY BOOKS

First published in the United States of America by
Rockport Publishers, Inc.
33 Commercial Street
Gloucester, Massachusetts 01930-5089
Telephone: (978) 282-9590
Facsimile: (978) 283-2742
www.rockpub.com

ISBN 1-56496-713-1
10 9 8 7 6 5 4 3 2 1

Design and Art Direction: Cathy Kelley
Layout: SYP Design & Production
Cover Image: Kevin Thomas
Photostyling: Cathy Kelley
Photography: Kevin Thomas

Printed in China.

contents

how to use this book

Painting Glass with the Color Shaper is a guide to creating colorful designs and patterns on glass surfaces by using color shaping techniques. Capture the luminosity and translucency of colored glass in just a few simple steps. Learn how to achieve unique transparent effects simulating molded and blown glass using Color Shapers and glass paints.

This book is designed to introduce you to an innovative approach to decorative painting on glass. You will become acquainted with the Color Shapers through basic exercises on glass sheets and 12 projects with easy-to-follow, step-by-step instructions, as well as pattern variations for each project. The projects draw inspiration from historical sources and interpret the characteristics of art glass in terms of color, design and pattern from ancient times to the present. The styles represented include ancient glass from the Mediterranean region, Islamic golden lustre glass, Venetian, Millefiori, Art Nouveau, Art Deco, and contemporary blown glass.

The glass objects for the projects presented are readily available in home goods stores, craft stores, and second-hand shops. Color Shaper sizes can be substituted if you do not have the size specified in the materials list. Combine imagination with color shaping, and discover a new and exciting alternative to decorative painting.

PALETTE Use the suggested palette or try mixing new color combinations.

CUTTING TEMPLATE Diagrams show how to notch the color shaper tools to attain the desired effect.

PATTERN SKETCHES A drawing is a helpful guide for the final piece.

STEP-BY-STEP INSTRUCTIONS The final patterns are achieved by following the steps.

basics

The patterns and designs featured on the glass projects in this book are created using the Color Shaper, an exciting new painting tool manufactured by Royal Sovereign, Ltd. Color shaping is a creative solution to traditional painting.

Color Shapers are rubber-tipped tools that come in a variety of sizes and shapes. The large Color Shapers speed up the decorative painting process by patterning large areas in a single stroke, while fine detail can be achieved with the smaller sizes. The concept behind color shaping is subtracting wet paint from the glass surface and leaving behind lines, marks and strokes. Combine simple strokes to create beautiful designs and unique effects. The Color Shaper's gray tip offers good control in wet paint. Clean the tip after use by dipping into soapy water or alcohol and wiping dry. In the projects that follow, you will discover the amazing effects of color shaping on glass, and with a little practice you will achieve polished results.

basic materials

Here is a list and description of some of the basic materials you will need to create
the projects that follow.

prepared surface	Degrease the glass surface with soapy water or alcohol.
Color Shapers	Rubber-tipped tools in various sizes and shapes that are used to carve images in wet paint.
brushes	In addition to Color Shapers, the projects use the following paint brushes: 1" (3 cm) soft wash brush, #12 flat shader brush, #1 and #4 script liners, and #8 round brush.
	Mixtique brushes by Loew-Cornelle are recommended, as they are designed specifically for glass painting; the natural bristles apply paint evenly, leaving behind no brushmarks. If these are not available at your local art and craft store, look for soft bristle brushes instead.
glass paint	The projects in this book use Pēbēo glass paints, Vitrea 160, transparent water-based paints for glass. The white and metallic gold paint used on projects in this book are from Pēbēo's Porcelain 150 collection, due to their opacity.
	Other transparent glass paints are available on the market. Carefully read the manufacturer's instructions.
extender	A drop (literally) of water mixed with glass paints will extend the open time, that is, the time in which the paint is wet and can be worked. To produce the color shaping effects, the paint must remain wet long enough to subtract the color.

baking guide

Color shaping involves a layering process. Each step must be protected before proceeding with the next layer. Follow these guidelines to ensure maximum results:

dry

Although the manufacturer's instructions say it is necessary for the paint to dry 24 hours before baking, or bubbling will occur, here is an alternative approach for speeding up the drying process: Place project in a cool oven, set at 150 degrees F (60C) for ten minutes. Turn the oven off, let the object cool and remove it from oven. This step simply dries the wet paint. This is an ideal temperature for drying because bubbling will not occur. (If you need to dry a painted stripe or brushstroke, you can simply use a hair dryer to blow it dry.)

dry and set

This step combines drying wet paint and heat setting for a tough finish before applying another layer of paint. Place project in a 150-degree F (60C) oven for ten minutes to dry. Increase the temperature to 325 degrees F (160C) and bake for 20 minutes. Turn oven off, cool down gradually and remove the object from oven. This process produces a sealed paint finish that is necessary before applying another layer of color.

final baking

Place completed project in cool oven and set at 150 degrees F (60C) for 10 minutes to dry the final layer of paint. Increase the temperature to 325 degrees F (160C) and bake for 30 minutes. Turn the oven off, cool down gradually and remove from oven. This final step produces a permanent paint finish and a functional surface.

beads and findings

Embellish painted glass with beads and findings. Colored glass beads and jewelry findings can enhance and add character to a painted glass object. In many instances, such embellishments can produce the finishing touch. Experiment by combining several types of beads to trim or accent your project.

Bead stores and crafts suppliers offer many different kinds of beads in a variety of sizes, shapes and colors. Ideally, a flat-backed bead is best suited for adhering to a glass surface. Use a glue or cement made for glass for the strongest adherence.

color shaper sizes and tips

This section presents the complete Color Shaper collection. The Color Shaper collection includes five distinct tips: Flat Chisel, Cup Round, Angle Chisel, Cup Chisel and Taper Point. Each tip comes in five sizes.

a   b   c

d   e

a. flat chisel   use for stripes and calligraphic strokes

b. cup round   use to carve short and long rounded strokes and petal forms

c. angle chisel   use the long sharp edge for broad strokes, tapered expressive strokes and leaf forms

d. cup chisel   use to adjust contours and edges

e. taper point   use for linear and broad marks

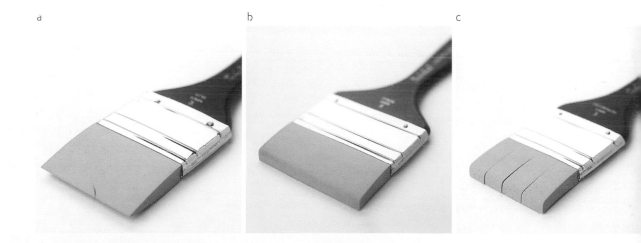

a   b   c

The Color Shaper Wide Collection includes three versatile tips: Flat Wide, Curve Wide and the Decorator. The sizes range from 1" (3 cm) to 3" (77 mm).

a. flat wide   use for large calligraphic strokes and a variety of wide stripes; may be cut and notched to create linear patterns

b. curve wide   use the sharp edge to carve wet paint cleanly; can be cut and notched to form striped patterns with very clean lines

c. decorator   use the pre-slit edge for creating soft linear patterns

basic brushstrokes

The range of Color Shaper sizes and tips can produce a wide variety of strokes from simple stripes and marks to calligraphic strokes. Here are some basic strokes that will appear in the following projects. Take some time to practice them on a sheet of glass. You can use the practice sheet of glass over and over by simply rinsing off the wet paint with soapy water. You will become familiar with the different techniques and get a feel for the proper consistency of the paint.

Flat Chisel

The Flat Chisel is used to create stripes, s-strokes, squiggles, curvilinear lines and angular marks.

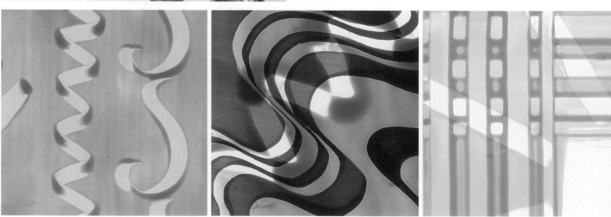

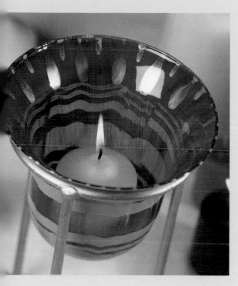

Curve Wide Color Shaper

The Curve Wide Color Shaper, cut and notched, makes its own distinctive mark. Customize the tips to create unique effects. The Curve Wide Color Shaper's sharp edge removes wet paint easily and when cut and notched creates clean stripes and lines, leaving behind no filmy residue on the glass surface. A few examples of linear patterns that will appear on projects are shown.

The Angle Chisel

The Angle Chisel is ideal for forming
leaf and pointed petal strokes.

Cup Round

The Cup Round is perfect for rounded petal strokes.

color shaping
on flat surfaces

WINDOW ORNAMENT · STRIPED FRAME · STORAGE CONTAINER · PERFUME BOTTLE · WINE DECANTER

A flat surface project is a great way to become acquainted with color shaping techniques. Begin with a two-dimensional surface or a flat-sided object. The featured window ornament and picture frame are ideal first projects because they are small and easy to handle.

Many of the same Color Shaper tips and sizes can be used with the flat surface projects that follow. Make sure you are equipped with the 1" (38mm) and 3" (77mm) Curve Wide, the #6 Cup Round, and #6 Flat Chisel Color Shapers to begin creating your beautiful designs.

As you become more familiar with color shaping techniques, try decorating flat-sided objects such as the storage container, perfume bottle, or wine decanter. These are great shapes to start with since each side can be done separately. Explore simple objects before progressing to the more complicated ones. Use the same method to color shape patterns on the glass. Begin with simple scalloped patterns and stripes, then try adding spirals, stripes, and squiggles. Then hold your creations up to the light, and watch as the melding of colors explodes in intricate patterns.

glowing window ornament

Glass window ornament

3" (77 mm) Curve Wide Color Shaper, cut and notched (see diagram)

1" (3 cm) soft wash brush

The beauty of colored glass is best revealed through filtered sunlight. A simple glass window ornament exposes glowing colors through illumination. This first project takes a triangular glass ornament and repeats a multicolored scalloped pattern. Turquoise, green, and yellow combine with translucent magenta to catch the sun, mirroring the multicolored glass rods used in contemporary blown glass. Add curves and spirals to create intricate patterns. Design several glowing ornaments of various shapes and sizes, then string them together to hang from a sunny window.

glass paint: yellow, green, turquoise, and magenta

▶ The 3" (77 mm) Curve Wide Color Shaper, cut and notched, creates the striped scallop pattern in a single stroke. If using a narrower width Color Shaper, you may have to repeat the step to finish the pattern. To vary your design, use the #6 Flat Chisel Color Shaper to form spiral shapes.

starting out

A simple line drawing on paper will help you to plan your design. Play with repetitive lines, scallops, and curves to form your pattern.

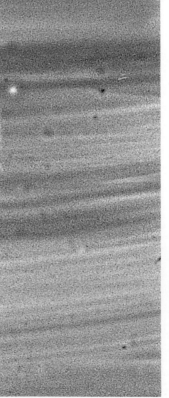

3

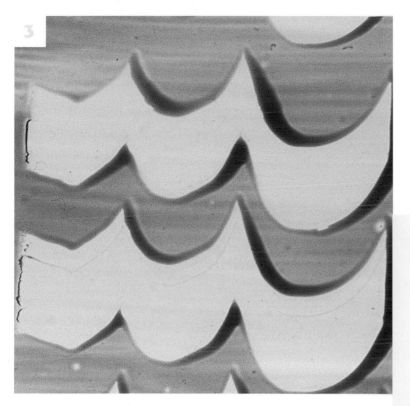

tip Try to apply the paint evenly with a light brush stroke to prevent ridged lines.

step one With the soft wash brush, make three stripes, in yellow, green, and turquoise to cover the entire background. Dry and set (see p. 7).

step two With a wash brush, apply a layer of magenta paint over prepared background.

step three Cut and notch the 3" (77 mm) Curve Wide Color Shaper (see diagram). Using the cut and notched Color Shaper, form a scalloped pattern in a single stroke. The size of the project makes it very easy to handle the technique. Follow final baking instructions in the basic materials section (see p. 7).

variations

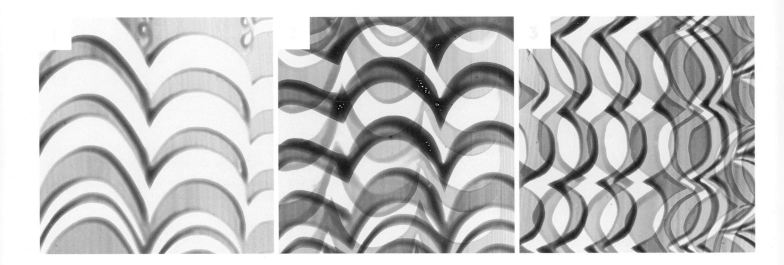

magenta and yellow scalloped design

Combine two layers of scalloped lines for a more complex pattern.

YOU WILL NEED

3" (77mm) Curve Wide Color Shaper, cut and notched (see diagram, p. 18)

#6 Flat Chisel Color Shaper

1" (3 cm) soft wash brush

glass paint: magenta, yellow

step one With the soft wash brush, apply a layer of magenta paint on the glass surface. With the cut and notched Curve Wide Color Shaper, make a scalloped pattern through the wet paint. Dry and set (see p. 7).

step two With the wash brush, apply yellow paint over the prepared basecoat. Using the cut and notched Curve Wide Color Shaper, make scalloped lines through the wet paint in the opposite direction. Notice the complex design that results from the intersection of the scalloped lines. Follow final baking instructions (see p. 7).

summer colored spirals

This variation features an underlying linear pattern with an overlay of simple spirals.

YOU WILL NEED

3" (77mm) Curve Wide Color Shaper, cut and notched (see diagram, p. 18)

#6 Flat Chisel Color Shaper

1" (3 cm) soft wash brush

glass paint: yellow, green, turquoise

step one With the wash brush, apply a layer of yellow-green over the glass surface. Using the cut and notched Color Shaper, form a curvilinear line through the wet paint. Dry and set (see p. 7).

step two The next step involves a second layer of color shaping. With the wash brush, apply a layer of turquoise paint over the prepared background. Using the #6 Flat Chisel Color Shaper, make spiral strokes through the wet paint to form an allover pattern. Follow final baking instructions.

MATERIALS

Glass frame

1-1/2" (38 mm) Curve
Wide Color Shaper, cut
and notched (see diagram)

#6 Flat Chisel Color
Shaper

1" (3 cm) soft wash brush

Glass marker: turquoise
(or you may use turquoise
paint with a liner brush)

Flat glass beads for
embellishing (optional)

stylish striped frame

Transform a simple square of glass into an objet d'art through color and pattern. The

interplay of citrus yellow with fuchsia combined with linear patterns leads to interest-

ing results. Contemporary blown glass is the reference point for this project, borrow-

ing inspiration from layers of transparent colors as seen in today's art glass. Choose a

frame with a smooth glass border. To create your own, rest two pieces of glass, cut to

size, on a plate stand or small easel. Paint and color shape the border, insert your

photo, and display your personalized piece of art on a mantle or shelf.

glass paint: lemon yellow, fuchsia, turquoise

▶ To produce clean intersecting lines of
color, use the 1-1/2" (38 mm) Curve Wide
Color Shaper, cut and notched. The #6 Flat
Chisel Color Shaper allows you to paint lines,
stripes, and zigzags for visual interest.

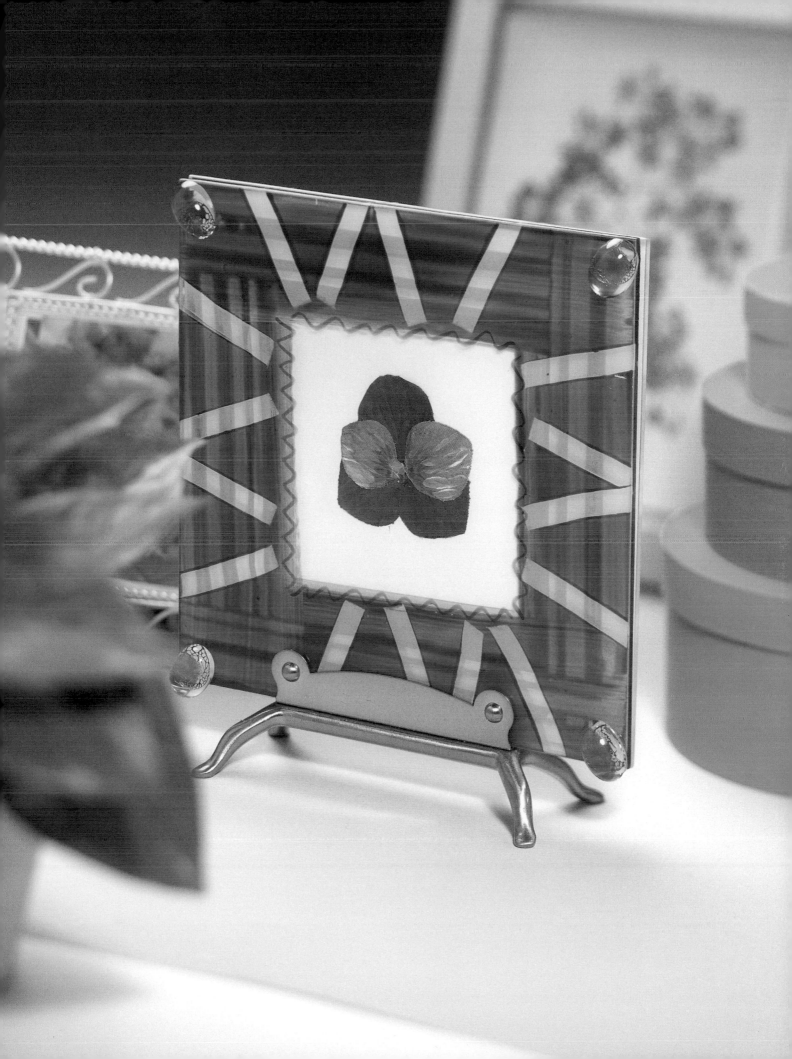

starting out

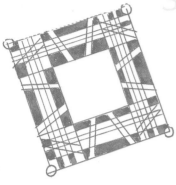

Plan the width of the border for the frame on a sheet of paper. Create a simple layout based on the measurements of the glass to secure your design concept. Vary the placement of the intersecting lines to enhance your pattern.

step one Using the 1 " (3 cm) wash brush, apply yellow paint (thinned with a drop of water) to the border areas of the frame. Apply paint to all four sides at the same time, to create intersecting lines in the four corners. Using the 1-1/2" Curve Wide Color Shaper, cut and notched, form stripes through the wet glaze on all four sides using firm pressure. Wipe the shaper as you go along. Notice the interesting patterns in the four corners where the lines intersect. Dry and set (see p. 7).

step two Apply the fuchsia paint (thinned with a drop of water) over the yellow layer. (You may do this step in sections, one side at a time.) Using the #6 Flat Chisel Color Shaper, form a series of lines through the wet paint, using firm pressure. Alternate directions to form a pattern. Notice the color changes as burnt orange becomes part of the palette.

3

step three Using the turquoise glass pen or turquoise paint with a liner brush, make a squiggly line, forming a square within the frame. Follow final baking instructions.

optional step Embellish the finished frame with beads.

Color coordinate your painted frame to enhance your favorite photo.

variations

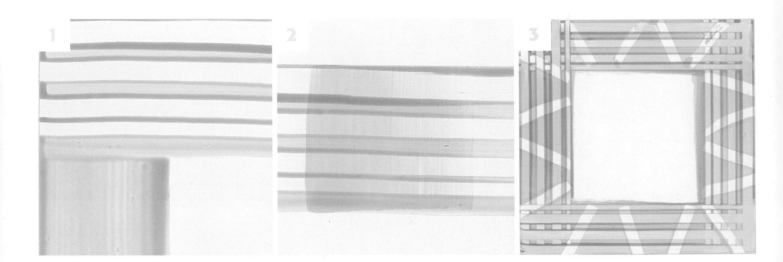

yellow and turquoise stripes

Keep the same pattern but change the color. Experiment with new and different color combinations. This pattern uses lemon yellow with light turquoise.

YOU WILL NEED

1 1/2" (38 mm) Curve Wide Color Shaper, cut and notched (see diagram, p. 24)

#6 Flat Chisel Color Shaper

1" (3 cm) soft wash brush

glass paint: turquoise, lemon yellow

step one   Using the 1" (3 cm) wash brush, apply light turquoise paint to form a border on all four sides of the frame. With the 1-1/2" (38 mm) Curve Wide Color Shaper, cut and notched, form stripes through the wet paint. Dry and set (see p. 7).

step two   With the wash brush, apply a coat of lemon yellow paint (thinned with a drop of water) over the turquoise stripes. Using the #6 Flat Chisel Color Shaper, make stripes through the wet paint to form a pattern. Complete all four sides. Follow final baking instructions.

tip You can do step two in sections.

fuchsia and turquoise zigzags

Create a more complex pattern by combining stripes with zigzags. This pattern combines two colors, fuchsia and turquoise.

YOU WILL NEED

1 1/2" (38 mm) Curve Wide Color Shaper, cut and notched (see diagram, p. 24)

1" (3 cm) soft wash brush

glass paint: fuschia, turquoise

step one With the 1" (3 cm) wash brush, apply a band of fuchsia paint, thinned with a drop of water, to form a border. Using the 1-1/2" (38 mm) Curve Wide Color Shaper, cut and notched, make stripes through the wet glaze. Dry and set (see p. 7).

step two With the 1" (3 cm) wash brush, apply a layer of turquoise paint, thinned with a drop of water, over the prepared border background. Using the 1-1/2" (38 mm) Curve Wide Color Shaper, cut and notched, make a zigzag pattern through the wet turquoise paint in the same direction of the stripes. Notice the interesting pattern that forms when the two colors interact. Follow final baking instructions (see p. 7).

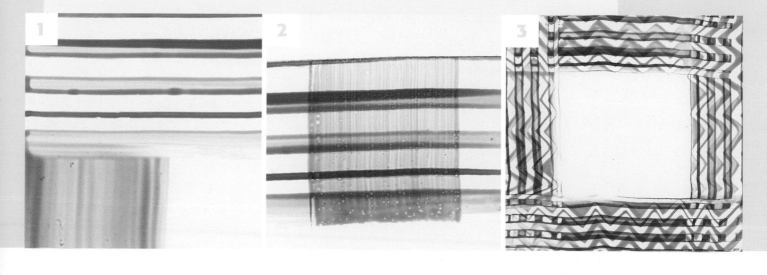

striking storage container

Combine beauty with utility in a series of painted glass storage containers. The combed linear pattern is an interpretation of ancient core-formed glass from the Mediterranean region. Spirals and intricate linear designs mirror the spirals of molten glass from this period. Turquoise, blue, and yellow reflect the colors typically used. Choose a box from a variety of heights and widths, then fill one with cotton puffs to accent your bathroom.

glass paint: turquoise

MATERIALS

Glass storage container

3" (77 mm) Curve Wide Color Shaper, cut and notched (see diagram) (You may substitute any of the other Wide Curve Color Shapers.)

1" (3 cm) soft wash brush

◀ The 3" (77 mm) Curve Wide Color Shaper cleanly removes the paint in one step. When you cut and notch the Color Shaper, clear stripes form wavy, zigzag, or combed patterns.

starting out

A quick sketch on paper will help you plan the direction of the combing and will solidify your design concept. Explore the width of the stripes, from narrow to broad. Customize the notched tip of your Color Shaper to reflect your design.

step one   With the 1" (3 cm) wash brush, apply turquoise paint, thinned with water, to the cover of the box. Using the 3" (77 mm) cut and notched Curve Wide Color Shaper, make wavy stripes through the wet glaze, applying firm pressure. If you use a narrow Shaper, you will have to repeat the step to cover the entire area.

tip Test the color shaping technique on a sheet of palette paper or a scrap piece of glass.

step two Continue applying paint and color shaping each side of the box, a section at a time. Follow final baking instructions.

variations

yellow, turquoise, and green combed pattern

You can enhance the turquoise pattern featured on the container by adding another layer of color. This pattern adds yellow, thereby producing green.

YOU WILL NEED

3" (77 mm) Curve Wide Color Shaper, cut and notched (see diagram, p. 31) (You may substitute any of the other Curve Wide Color Shapers.)

1" (3 cm) soft wash brush

glass paint: turquoise, yellow

step one   Create the turquoise pattern outlined in the main project, and dry and set it (see p. 7).

step two   With a soft wash brush, apply yellow paint, thinned with water, over the turquoise pattern. Do each section of the box separately. With the 3" (77 mm) Curve Wide Color Shaper, cut and notched, comb through the wet paint using a curving movement in the opposite direction of the design in the turquoise. Notice the interesting transparent effects. Follow final baking instructions.

mediterranean stripes

Keeping in the tradition of the Mediterranean colors, this variation uses a yellow and ultramarine color combination with a zigzag pattern.

tip Remove wet paint from the Color Shaper as you go along. The paint tends to accumulate in the curve.

YOU WILL NEED

3" (77 mm) Curve Wide Color Shaper, cut and notched (see diagram, p. 31)

1" (3 cm) soft wash brush

glass paint: ultramarine, yellow

step one   With the 1" (3 cm) wash brush, apply ultramarine paint, thinned with water, to the container cover first and then to each side of the box. Using the 3" (77 mm) Curve Wide Color Shaper, cut and notched, form a zigzag pattern through the wet glaze, using firm pressure. Dry and set this step (see p. 7).

step two   Using a wash brush, apply yellow paint, thinned with water, over the blue background, doing the top and sides separately. With the 3" (77 mm) Curve Wide Color Shaper, cut and notched, form straight stripes through the wet glaze. Notice the color interaction when yellow overlaps blue. Color shape all sides of box to complete the pattern. Follow final baking instructions.

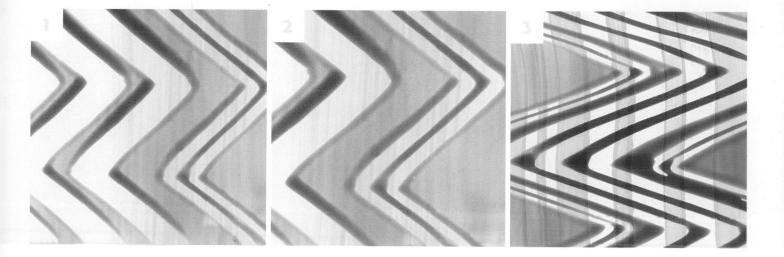

elegant perfume bottle

Glass perfume bottle

1-1/2" (38 mm) Curve Wide Color Shaper, cut and notched (see diagram) (other sizes may be substituted)

#6 Cup Round Color Shaper

1" (3 cm) soft wash brush

#4 script liner brush

The perfume bottle translates the characteristics of contemporary Venetian glass. The role of color is emphasized and careful consideration is given to tint, composition and depth. The project combines translucent color with opaque areas. Notice the interplay of light through the striped blue areas. The design can be easily adapted to fit other bottle shapes. For instance, if the stopper is smaller, you might try incorporating the black and white pattern somewhere on the bottle itself.

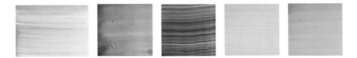

glass paint: azure blue, deep blue-violet, black, white, and gold

▶ Vertical and diagonal lines are clearly defined with the 1-1/2" (38 mm) Curve Wide Color Shaper, cut and notched for a series of stripes. Use the #6 Cup Round Color Shaper to create rounded petal strokes.

starting out   Sketch the bottle on

paper to assess its shape. Organize the design elements to fit the form of the bottle. Vary the pattern by

changing the width of the stripes, from a delicate to a bold pattern.

step one Apply a thin coat of azure blue, thinned with a drop of water, over the entire bottle. Dry and set (see p. 7).

step two Using a 1" (3 cm) wash brush, apply the deep blue-violet paint, thinned with a drop of water, over the prepared basecoat in sections. Pull the 1-1/2" (38 mm) Curve Wide Color Shaper, cut and notched, through the wet paint, using firm pressure, to make stripes.

step three Apply an even coat of white paint over the entire stopper, using the 1" (3 cm) wash brush. Dry and set.

When creating the petal stroke with the Cup Round Color Shaper, push down and away into the wet paint using firm pressure. Keep the pressure at the tip of the Shaper.

4

3

step four Using the 1" (3 cm) wash brush, apply black paint, thinned with a drop of water, over the cooled white paint in sections. With the #6 Cup Round Color Shaper, form short petal strokes by pushing away through the wet paint. Accent with gold using the # 4 script liner brush. Follow final baking instructions.

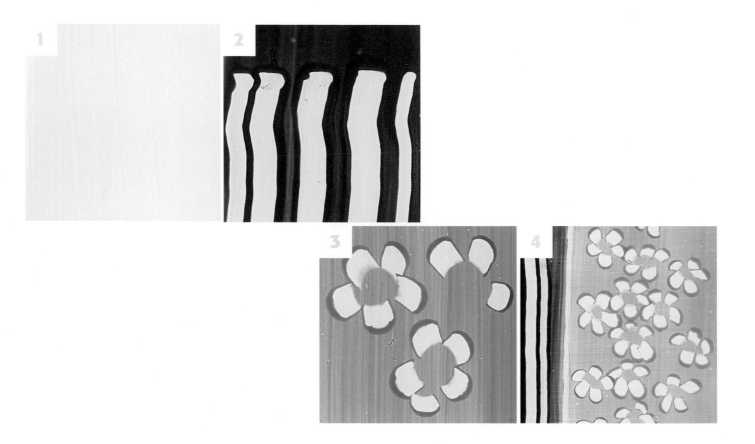

turquoise petals with bold stripes

This variation redefines the role of black and white. The stripes are black and white while turquoise is introduced into the petal shapes.

YOU WILL NEED

1 1/2" (38 mm) Curve Wide Color Shaper, cut and notched (see diagram, p. 36)

#6 Cup Round Color Shaper

1" (3 cm) soft wash brush

glass paint: white, black, turquoise

step one   Apply a basecoat of white paint using the 1" (3 cm) soft wash brush to the bottle and stopper. Dry and set (see p. 7).

step two   On the bottle, use the 1" wash brush to apply a layer of black paint over the prepared white background. Using the 1-1/2" (38 mm) Curve Wide Color Shaper, cut and notched, make vertical stripes through the wet black paint. Set aside.

step three On the stopper, use the 1" (3 cm) wash brush to apply turquoise paint, thinned with a drop of water, over the white background. Using the #6 Cup Round Color Shaper, make petal shapes, creating small flowers, in the wet paint. Pushing away with the rounded tip will form the petal. Place the bottle and stopper in a cool oven and follow the final baking instructions.

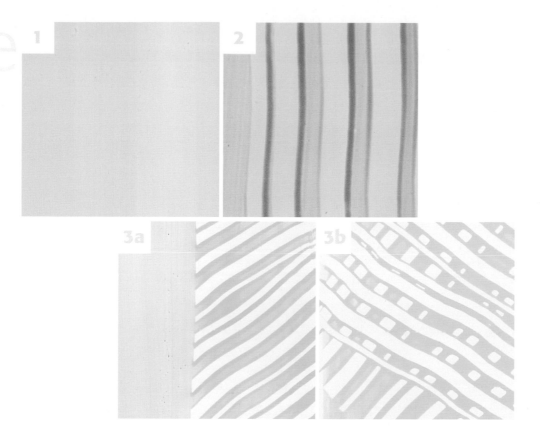

yellow and red crisscross design

This variation features a yellow and red color combination but it also uses the glass as part of the special effects. Notice where the yellow paint is subtracted, leaving behind areas of clear glass.

YOU WILL NEED

1 1/2" (38 mm) Curve Wide Color Shaper, cut and notched (see diagram, p. 36) (You may substitute the 1" (3 cm) Curve Wide color Shaper, cut and notched)

1" (3 cm) soft wash brush

glass paint: yellow, red

step one With the 1" (3 cm) soft wash brush, apply a layer of yellow paint over sides of bottle. Dry and set (see p. 7).

step two With a 1" (3 cm) soft wash brush, apply red paint, thinned with a drop of water, over prepared yellow background, in sections. Using the 1-1/2" (38 mm) Curve Wide Color Shaper, cut and notched, make vertical stripes in the wet paint. Set aside.

step three A With the 1" (3 cm) wash brush, apply a layer of yellow paint over stopper area. Using the 1-1/2" (38 mm) Curve Wide Color Shaper (or the 1" (3 cm) Curve Wide Color Shaper), cut and notched, make a series of diagonal lines through the wet paint.

step three B Immediately then make a crisscross design with the cut and notched Color Shaper by making diagonal lines in the opposite direction. The pattern is complete. Note the effects created when the yellow paint is subtracted leaving behind areas of natural glass. Follow the final baking instructions.

colorful wine decanter

A beautifully painted decanter can serve as a showpiece on your table. Use the decanter to serve wine or ice water to dinner-party guests. The interaction of vibrant colors and latticework recalls the 19th century art of interweaving multi-colored glass rods. Yellow, white, and turquoise form the underlayer of color, while magenta twists are color shaped to create a lattice effect.

MATERIALS

Glass wine decanter

#6 Flat Chisel Color Shaper

1" (3 cm) soft wash brush

#4 script liner brush

#8 round brush

#12 flat shader

glass paints: white, yellow, magenta, and turquoise

The #6 Flat Chisel Color Shaper helps you to easily create the twisted lattice pattern, forming twists and squiggle lines through the paint. Use the 3" (77 mm) Curve Wide Color Shaper, cut and notched, to vary your design with diagonal lines.

starting out

Plan your design on a sketch of the decanter to see how the edges will come together. Play with the width of the stripes using brushes of various sizes.

step one   Using the wash brush, paint vertical stripes in white on all four sides. Dry with a hair dryer. With the #12 flat shader brush, paint a series of horizontal stripes in light yellow (yellow mixed with white) over the white on all four sides. Blow dry.

step two   With the #4 script liner, form a series of narrow vertical stripes in light turquoise (turquoise mixed with white). Dry and set (see p. 7).

step three With the wash brush, apply an even layer of magenta over the plaid background. Using the #6 Flat Chisel Color Shaper, form a series of diagonal twists first in one direction, then immediately in the opposite direction. Accent top portion and stopper in yellow and magenta, adding a few petal strokes around the stopper. Follow final baking instructions.

tip Practice twisted lattice strokes on palette paper or glass sheet first. Simply move the #6 Flat Chisel Color Shaper back and forth in the wet paint to form a squiggle line.

variations

blue and purple latticework

This pattern features a simple twisted cross band pattern in a two color combination.

YOU WILL NEED

3" (77 mm) Curve Wide Color Shaper, cut and notched (see diagram, p. 50)

#6 Flat Chisel Color Shaper

1" (3 cm) soft wash brush

glass paint: blue, white, purple

step one With a wash brush, apply a layer of light blue (blue mixed with white) over the glass surface. With the 3" (77 mm) Curve Wide Color Shaper, cut and notched, make diagonal lines through the wet paint. Dry and set (see p. 7).

step two With the wash brush, apply a layer of purple paint over the prepared basecoat. Using the #6 Flat Chisel Color Shaper, form a series of lattice twists through the wet paint, first in one diagonal direction and then immediately in the opposite direction. Follow final baking instructions.

fiery waves and latticework

This pattern features a curvilinear pattern as the underlayer.

YOU WILL NEED

3" (77 mm) Curve Wide Color Shaper, cut and notched (see diagram, p. 50)

#6 Flat Chisel Color Shaper

1" (3 cm) soft wash brush

glass paint: red, white, orange

step one   Prepare pink paint (red mixed with white). With the wash brush, apply the pink layer over the glass surface. With the 3" (77 mm) Curve Wide Color Shaper, cut and notched, form a series of wavy lines through the wet paint in one diagonal direction. Dry and set (see p. 7).

step two   With the wash brush, apply a layer of orange over the prepared background. Using the #6 Flat Chisel Color Shaper, create lattice twists, forming a cross band design. Follow final baking instructions.

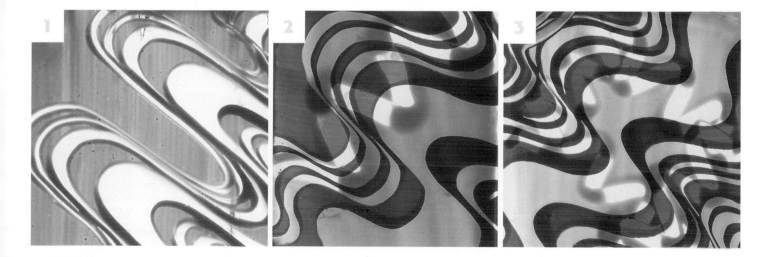

color shaping on rounded surfaces

CANDLE HOLDER · CANDY DISH · POURING PITCHER · VASE · SHALLOW BOWL · CAKE DOME · MILLEFIORI BOWL

Rounded glass objects such as vases, bowls, candy dishes, jars, pitchers, and candle holders make excellent projects for glass painting. Keep in mind that handling the object can be a little bit tricky. You will need to use one hand to hold and turn the project and the other to apply the glaze and do the color shaping. This will ensure continuity in paint application and enable you to accomplish the techniques successfully.

Flea markets, second-hand shops and home goods stores can provide numerous glass objects such as bottles, sugar bowls and creamers, butter dishes, and cruet sets. You will discover unlimited possibilities as you search for projects and transform ordinary shapes into works of art. If you use your imagination and are resourceful, you can create unique pieces for the home, or perhaps even develop a gift product line.

iridescent candle holder

MATERIALS

Glass candle holder

3" (77 mm) Curve Wide
Color Shaper, cut and
notched (see template)

1" (3 cm) soft wash brush

#4 script liner brush

Ribbon patterns, curvilinear designs, and iridescent colors best describe Art Nouveau glass. You will find many vases in the Art Nouveau style, often decorated with complex floral patterns and decorative ribbon-like designs. This project uses curvilinear patterns to transform a simple shape into a style characterized by Art Nouveau design. Combining transparent colors with opaque colors creates dramatic effects. Candle holders are very popular and can be found in numerous sizes and shapes from small table accents to large, floor-size holders. The general rule with glass candle holders is not to let the flame burn down to the very bottom.

glass paints: violet, blue-violet, white, and gold

▶ The 3" (77 mm) Curve Wide Color Shaper, cut and notched, forms a series of broad repetitive lines in a single stroke. Vary your strokes to create a scalloped or ribbon pattern.

starting out

A scale drawing of your candle holder will help you identify the best areas to color shape. You will get a better sense of design possibilities by plotting your ideas on paper. Draw repeated lines in a curvilinear direction to form a pattern.

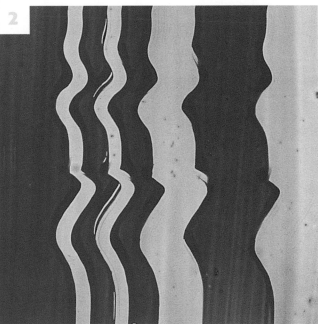

step one   With the wash brush, apply an even layer of transparent violet paint over the entire surface. Dry and set (see p. 7).

step two   Apply a layer of light blue-violet paint (blue-violet mixed with white) evenly over the entire surface. Thin the paint with a single drop of water. Using the 3" (77 mm) Curve Wide Color Shaper, cut and notched, form a wavy line through the wet paint. Try to match the lines as you come to the end. You can stop half way, wipe the tip and get a better grip for the second half of the project. Dry and set.

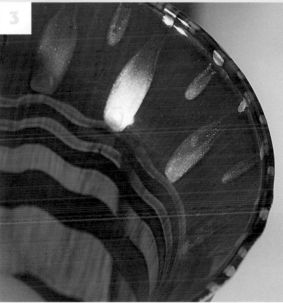

tip

Keep the paint wet long enough to complete the stripe.

step three Using the #4 script liner brush,, create a striped border in metallic gold around the inside lip of the candle holder. Form straight strokes spaced evenly all around the edge. Notice the interesting contrast between transparency and opacity when you hold it up to the light. Follow final baking instructions.

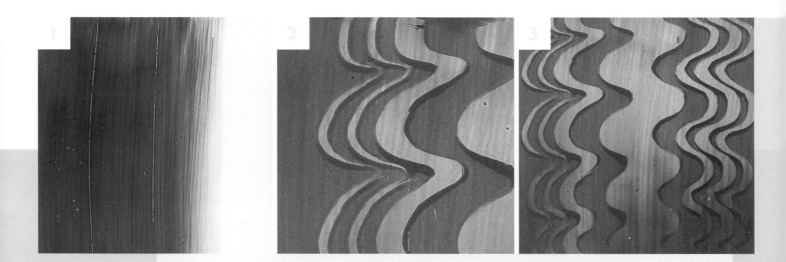

violet scalloped linear pattern

This variation uses a repetitive curvilinear line to form the pattern. The 3" (77 mm) Curve Wide Color Shaper, cut and notched, forms the pattern instantly.

YOU WILL NEED

3" (77 mm) Curve Wide Color Shaper, cut and notched (see diagram, p. 50)

1" (3 cm) soft wash brush

glass paint: red, violet, white

step one   With the wash brush apply a thin layer of red-violet paint over the entire surface of the project. Dry and set (see p.7).

step two   Apply an even coat of light violet (violet mixed with white) over the entire surface. Thin the paint with a single drop of water. Using the 3" (77 mm) Curve Wide Color Shaper, cut and notched, form a curved line through the wet paint. Follow final baking instructions.

purple and gold ribbon pattern

The ribbon pattern is representative of Art Nouveau decoration. It features the ribbon design against a metallic gold background, recalling the iridescent qualities of the Art Nouveau style.

YOU WILL NEED

3" (77 mm) Curve Wide Color Shaper, cut and notched (see diagram, p. 50)

1" (3 cm) soft wash brush

glass paint: gold, purple

step one   With a soft wash brush, apply a layer of metallic gold over the entire surface of the project. Dry and set (see p. 7).

step two   Apply a layer of deep purple paint, thinned with a single drop of water, over the prepared surface. With the 3" (77 mm)Curve Wide Color Shaper, cut and notched, make a bracketed stroke through the wet glaze, creating the ribbon pattern. If you should stop, be sure to start again where you left off. Follow final baking instructions.

lustrous candy dish

MATERIALS

Glass candy dish

#6 Angle Chisel Color Shaper

1" (3 cm) soft wash brush

#4 script liner brush

#10 flat brush

The golden hue of this candy dish has its origins in the ancient tradition of Islamic craftsmen, who applied a metallic powder to glass and ceramics, creating lustre glass.

This project interprets the qualities of golden lustre with luminous effects. Using a wash to recreate the translucent golden glow, a series of ferns is then color shaped onto the dish. A sugar bowl can be substituted for a candy dish.

glass paint: white, turquoise, and gold

▷ Form a series of ferns using the angled edge of the #6 Angle Chisel Color Shaper. The long, sharp edge is ideal for broad or tapered leaf strokes.

Begin with a sketch. Organize a couple of simple leaf designs on paper to form a repetitive pattern. A layout will help arrange the spacing. A single leaf can be repeated, or combine a cluster of leaves to form a design.

step one Using the wash brush, apply a thin layer of turquoise paint over the entire candy dish, cover and bottom. You will achieve a transparent effect. Dry and set (see p. 7).

step two Mix white and turquoise to form a light turquoise. Using the #10 flat brush, combine three s-strokes to create a leaf motif. Repeat this step to complete the border pattern around both pieces of glass. Dry and set.

step three Using the wash brush, apply a layer of gold paint over candy dish. With the #6 Angle Chisel Color Shaper, form a series of ferns through the wet paint. Use the angled edge of the shaper and push away forming a stroke mark. Clean the tip as you go along. Repeat this step on the cover.

step four Using the #4 script liner brush, paint metallic gold stripes around the bottom of the bowl. Follow final baking instructions.

golden fern with turquoise

You can also create a lustre effect by reversing the order of color. This pattern starts with a gold background then overlays turquoise, leaving behind a gold fern pattern.

YOU WILL NEED

#6 Angle Chisel Color Shaper

1" (3 cm) soft wash brush

glass paint: gold, turquoise

step one Using the wash brush, apply an even coat of metallic gold paint over the entire surface.
Dry and set (see p. 7).

step two Apply a thin layer of turquoise paint over the prepared gold surface. Using the #6 Angle Chisel Color Shaper, make a series of ferns through the wet paint. Notice the brilliant golden ferns that appear. Follow final baking instructions.

multiple leaf design

This patterns features a more complex leaf using the same s-stroke, and a burnt-orange overlayer in place of the turquoise.

YOU WILL NEED

#6 Angle Chisel Color Shaper

#10 flat bursh

1" (3 cm) soft wash brush

glass paint: gold, orange, turquoise

step one   Using the soft wash brush, apply an even layer of metallic gold over the glass surface. Dry and set (see p. 7).

step two   Load the #10 flat brush with light turquoise (turquoise mixed with white) to form a leaf by combining a series of s-strokes. Begin by painting the center stroke. On each side of this stroke form a series of three similar strokes

decreasing in size. Keep symmetry in mind as you build the leaf. Dry and set.

step three   With the 1" (3 cm) wash brush, apply a layer of burnt orange paint over the prepared surface. Using the #6 Angle Chisel Color Shaper, make a series of ferns by subtracting color between each painted leaf. You will see a complex pattern emerge.

dramatic pouring pitcher

Place this beautifully painted pitcher on a bright shelf or tabletop to display the luminous plaid of red and yellow. Hints of pink and orange are revealed as light shines through the glass. The intersecting diagonal lines of this design are interpreted from a 20th century Italian glass-making technique, Scozzese, or "Scottish," for its tartan-like qualities. The glass process involved criss-crossing inlaid rods of different colored glass. Use the color shaping techniques to create this effect with paint.

glass paint: yellow, white, and red.

MATERIALS

Glass pitcher

1-1/2" (38 mm) Curve Wide Color Shaper, cut and notched (see diagram) (This pattern uses two different cut and notched tips for a varied effect; however, you can work with the same tip if you wish.)

1" (3 cm) wash brush

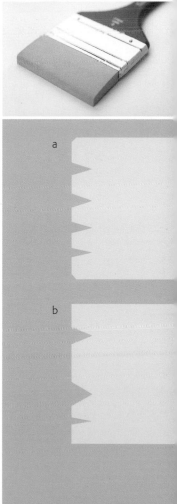

a

b

◀ Apply firm pressure to the 1-1/2" (38 mm) Curve Wide Color Shaper, cut and notched, to achieve clean, diagonal lines. Use two different cut and notched tips to create intersecting lines of various dimensions. To vary your design, use the 3" (77 mm) Curve Wide Color Shaper, cut and notched, to form a wider criss-cross of lines.

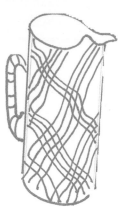

Plan the direction of the lines and form the plaid first in the form of a sketch. To vary the width of the plaid, customize your cut and notched Curve Wide Color Shaper to reflect your design.

step one With the wash brush, apply a layer of light yellow (yellow mixed with white, and thinned with a drop of water) glass paint over the entire pitcher. This application needs to be done in one step. Using the 1-1/2" (38 mm) Curve Wide Color Shaper, cut and notched, make a series of diagonal lines in one direction through the wet paint. Use firm pressure when color shaping to achieve nice clean lines. Cover the entire pitcher with a lined pattern. Dry and set (see p. 7).

step two With the wash brush, apply a layer of red paint, thinned with a drop of water, over the entire yellow striped background.

step three Using the 1-1/2" (38 mm) Curve Wide Color Shaper, cut and notched, make a series of diagonal lines in the opposite direction. Use the second cut and notched tip here to vary the effect. Follow final baking instructions.

tip Find a comfortable way to hold the pitcher so that you can create continuous, clean lines.

variations

multicolored plaid

This variation takes the yellow and red plaid a step further by adding an overlay of turquoise. The results are quite interesting when held to the light.

YOU WILL NEED

3" (77 mm) Curve Wide Color Shaper, cut and notched (see diagram, p. 50)

1 1/2" (38 mm) Curve Wide Color Shaper, cut and notched (see diagram, p. 63)

1" (3 cm) soft wash brush

glass paint: yellow, white, red, turquoise

step one Complete the yellow and red plaid and finish as directed, and dry and set (see p. 7). With the wash brush, apply a layer of turquoise paint over the entire glass pitcher. Using the 1-1/2" (38 mm) Curve Wide Color Shaper, cut and notched, make additional diagonal lines through the wet paint. Notice the color changes that occur—yellow turns to green, and red turns to burgundy.

blue and yellow plaid

Explore other color combinations. This pattern features a light blue with yellow-orange.

YOU WILL NEED

3" (77 mm) Curve Wide Color Shaper, cut and notched (see diagram, p. 50) (This variation uses two different cut and notched tips for a varied effect; however, you can work with the same tip if you wish.)

1" (3 cm) soft wash brush

glass paint: blue, white, yellow, orange

step one With the wash brush, apply a layer of light blue (blue mixed with white, and thinned with a single drop of water) glass paint over the entire pitcher. This application needs to be done in one step. Using the 3" (77mm) Curve Wide Color Shaper, cut and notched, create diagonal stripes through the wet paint. Dry and set.

step two With the wash brush, apply a layer of yellow-orange paint (thinned with a drop of water) over the entire prepared background. Using the 3" (77 mm) Curve Wide Color Shaper with a different cut and notched tip, make diagonal stripes in the opposite direction. Follow final baking instructions.

semi-abstract **vase**

MATERIALS

Glass vase

#6 Angle Chisel Color
Shaper (other sizes may
be substituted)

#10 Cup Round Color
Shaper (other sizes may
be substituted)

1" (3 cm) soft wash brush

#4 script liner brush

#12 flat brush

The interaction of color and pattern characterizes Art Deco, where semi-abstract design elements are drawn from natural plant forms such as leaves, flowers, fruits, berries, etc. The palette of vibrant yellow and turquoise is inspired by the rich colors of Art Deco design. New colors emerge as the colors overlap. The pattern featured here uses a semi-abstract flower to form the overall pattern. A few simple brush-strokes create the flower shape. Brushstrokes combined with color shaping techniques result in a complex pattern.

glass paint: white, yellow, and turquoise

▶ Forming long and short rounded strokes, the #10 Cup Round Color Shaper creates perfect petal shapes. Use the long, sharp edge of the #6 Angle Chisel Color Shaper to pattern a zigzag line. To vary your design, use the 1-1/2" (38 mm) Curve Wide Color Shaper, cut and notched, to achieve a clear, scalloped flower.

starting out

Collect some ideas by researching Art Deco designs. There are many books on the subject with wonderful colored patterns. Experiment with one or two simple design elements and apply them to a scaled drawing of your project. Consider placement and spacing. This pattern uses basic strokes to form the underlying design.

step one A repetitive design made up of basic strokes is the underlying pattern for this project. Simple strokes such as a c-stroke and comma strokes are combined to form the repeating motif. Use your imagination and combine strokes to form a design. For this project, make a c-stroke in white with the 1" (3 cm) wash brush to form the heart of the design. Form comma strokes with the #12 flat brush, and short strokes with the #4 script liner. Dry and set (see p. 7).

step two Using the 1" (3 cm) wash brush and #12 flat brush, create additional c-strokes and s-strokes in yellow, spilling on to the previous white strokes. Dry and set.

These steps are easy to do because you can do them in sections, completing the pattern as you go along.

step three A Using the 1" (3 cm) wash brush, create a c-stroke in turquoise over the base c-stroke. With the #10 Cup Round Color Shaper, form petals through the wet paint, pushing away. Notice the interesting effects where the yellow and white show through.

step three B Create s-strokes in turquoise with the 1" (3 cm) wash brush, overlaying the previous comma strokes. With the #6 Angle Chisel Color Shaper, form a zigzag line through the wet paint. Follow final baking instructions.

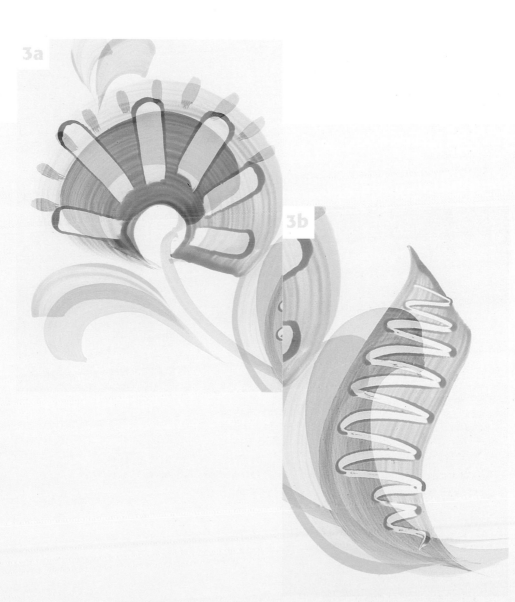

variations

tossed floral pattern

This pattern takes basic brush strokes and forms smaller motifs, applying them in a random, "tossed" placement. The basic flower shape is a combination of three c-strokes that are joined to form one shape.

YOU WILL NEED

#10 Cup Round Color Shaper

#6 Angle Chisel Color Shaper

#12 flat brush

#1 script liner brush

1" (3 cm) soft wash brush

glass paint: turquoise, yellow, orange

step one   Using the #12 flat brush, apply turquoise paint to create a series of flower shapes in a random pattern. Add stem strokes to the flowers with the #1 script liner brush. Dry and set (see p. 7).

step two   Using a 1" (3 cm) soft wash brush, apply yellow-orange paint, thinned with water, over the design (you can do this in sections if you wish). With the #10 Cup Round Color Shaper, form petal strokes though the wet paint over each of the underlying flower shapes. Using the #6 Angle Chisel Color Shaper, form spirals through the wet paint. Follow final baking instructions.

linear flowers

This pattern presents a flower of the same shape but uses a different painting approach.

YOU WILL NEED

1 1/2" (38 mm) Curve Wide Color Shaper, cut and notched (see diagram, p. 63) (You may use another size Curve Wide Color Shaper)

#10 Cup Round Color Shaper

1" (3 cm) soft wash brush

glass paint: turquoise, white, red, violet

step one   With the 1" (3 cm) wash brush, apply a layer of light turquoise paint (turquoise mixed with white), thinned with a drop of water, over the glass surface. Using the 1-1/2" (38 mm) (or other size) Curve Wide Color Shaper, cut and notched, make a scalloped flower in the wet paint. Clean the shaper as you go along. Dry and set (see p. 7).

step two   Using the 1" (3 cm) wash brush, apply red-violet paint, thinned with a drop of water, over the prepared background. With the #10 Cup Round Color Shaper, make petal strokes through the wet paint. Push down and away with the shaper to create the stroke. Clean the tip as you go along. Follow final baking instructions.

vibrant sunflower pattern bowl

A shallow glass bowl is an ideal way to display favorite collections, such as seashells or sea glass. Or color it with vivid paints and display in a sunny window. This glass bowl is painted with luminous colors inspired by the vibrant hues of contemporary blown glass. A semi-abstract floral design is repeated to create an overall pattern. Half-circle shapes form the underlayer of the flower. For this project, choose a glass bowl that has a flat brimmed edge to work well as a border area. Use it to hold wrapped candy or the day's mail. Contact with food is not recommended.

MATERIALS

Glass bowl

#6 Flat Chisel Color Shaper

1" (25 mm) soft wash brush

#4 script liner brush

#8 round brush

Flat glass beads

glass paints: white, yellow, turquoise, orange, blue-violet, and red

◀ The #6 Flat Chisel Color Shaper creates simple short and long lines and squiggles. Applying the Color Shaper back and forth over the sunflower petals melds colors together and creates new ones.

starting out

Create a design

layout on paper first. Draw a large circle, representing the bowl. Repeat a series

of small semi-circles to form the border and inside section. To give an

idea of placement and spacing, add squiggles over the semi-circles,

suggesting the color shaping technique.

step one Create the underpainting that consists of base semi-circles in yellow outlined in turquoise. Mix white and yellow paint together to make a light yellow. Load the 1" (25 mm) wash brush with yellow paint and form a series of half circles to create the border and inside section. Next, mix white and turquoise together. With the #4 script liner brush, outline each of the circles using a single stroke of the brush. Dry and set (see p. 7).

step two Using the #8 round brush, paint petal strokes in orange over each of the semi-circles and in blue-violet between the circles. Practice the strokes on paper first to get an idea of the amount of pressure on the brush. This completes the underpainting step. Dry and set.

step three Using the wash brush, apply transparent pink paint (red mixed with white), thinned with a single drop of water, over the prepared background in sections. With the #6 Flat Chisel Color Shaper, make zigzags in the wet glaze over each of the circles. Using firm pressure, move the Color Shaper back and forth, subtracting the wet glaze. Clean the tip as you go along. You may wish to practice this step on a piece of scrap glass first. Notice the interesting color changes that occur. Continue this process until the entire bowl is color shaped.

step four Compete the pattern by painting small petal strokes in gold using the #4 script liner brush. Follow final baking instructions.

tip Practice making the half-circle stroke. A clean sweep of the brush will give a quality stroke with no ridges.

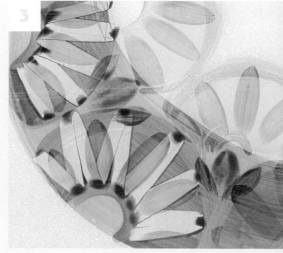

variations

blue and white sunflower

Several shades of blue animate this monochromatic variation on the sunflower pattern.

YOU WILL NEED

#6 Flat Chisel Color Shaper

#4 script liner

1" (3 cm) soft wash brush

glass paint: white, blue

step one   Using the 1" (3 cm) wash brush, form the semi-circle brush strokes in white. Outline each stroke in light blue (blue mixed with white) using the #4 script liner brush. This completes the underpainting. Dry and set (see p. 7).

step two   Using a soft wash brush, apply the blue paint over the prepared background in sections forming a band. With the #6 Flat Chisel Color Shaper, make zigzags in the wet glaze to create the petals. Color shape the entire surface. Follow final baking instructions.

golden sunflower

You can achieve elegance by simply limiting your palette to metallic gold. The combination of clear glass and metallic gold creates brilliant, luminous effects.

YOU WILL NEED

#6 Flat Chisel Color Shaper

#6 Angle Chisel Color Shaper

1" (3 cm) soft wash brush

glass paint: gold

step one Using a wash brush, paint a gold band to form the border.

step two With the #6 Flat Chisel Color Shaper, form zigzags into the wet paint to create the petals. Color shape the entire border.

step three Apply the gold in the center section of the bowl and form a crisscross pattern using the #6 Angle Chisel Color Shaper. Follow final baking instructions.

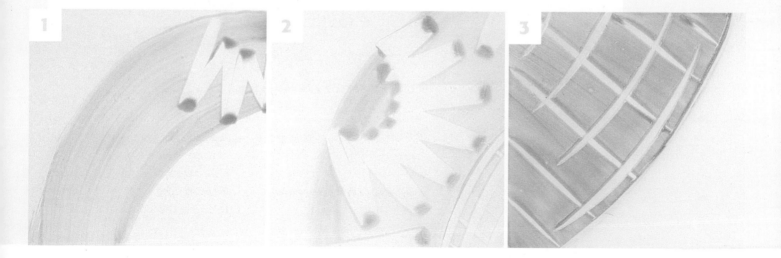

exotic cake dome

MATERIALS

Glass cake dome with pedestal

#6 Angle Chisel Color Shaper

1" (3 cm) wash brush

#12 flat shader brush

#4 script liner brush

#1 script liner brush

Create a unique yet familiar pattern as you rely on the shapes of nature for inspiration. The repeating leaf design produces a colorful, abstract motif, representative of the Art Deco period. Choose an unusual leaf or seashell to create your design. Repeat the shape to form a decorative pattern. A leaf design is repeated here to form a border around the dome as well as on the pedestal base. Portions of the dome are left clear to reveal that special dessert stored within. You can substitute a cheese dome for a smaller project.

glass paints: white, turquoise, yellow, and magenta

▶ Use the long, sharp edge of the #6 Angle Chisel Color Shaper to run zigzag lines over each leaf design. Use other Colors Shapers to vary your art; the #6 Cup Round forms rounded strokes and petal shapes, and the 3" (77 mm) Curve Wide, cut and notched, cleanly forms wavy stripes.

starting out

Select a single design element (this project features a leaf but you can experiment with other motifs) and repeat it to form a pattern. Prepare a simple sketch to secure your concept. Try varying the size of your leaf or other design element for even more visual interest.

step one A Use the 1" (3 cm) wash brush and the #12 flat shader brush to create an alternating leaf pattern in white by varying the sizes of the leaves. Form leaf strokes around the sides of the dome and at the base of the pedestal.

step one B Using the #12 flat shader brush, overlay small leaf strokes on top of the white using a light turquoise (turquoise mixed with white). Outline each leaf using the #4 script liner brush (or a 1" script liner). Dry and set (see p. 7).

step two With the wash brush, apply yellow paint over the prepared pattern. Using the #6 Angle Chisel Color Shaper, form a zigzag line through the wet paint on each leaf. Use the #1 script liner brush to edge the border with a squiggly line. This completes the bottom portion of the dome and pedestal.

step three With the wash brush, paint a series of scalloped strokes in white around the top of the dome. Add an s-stroke between each scallop using the #12 flat shader brush.

step four A With the #4 script liner brush, paint a series of linear leaf strokes in light turquoise. Dry and set.

step four B With the wash brush, apply a yellow band over the prepared background. Using the #6 Angle Chisel Color Shaper, make a series of zigzags through the wet paint. At this time, accent the very top portion of dome, lip, and pedestal in magenta. Follow final baking instructions.

tip
You can apply the yellow paint layer and color shape this pattern in sections.

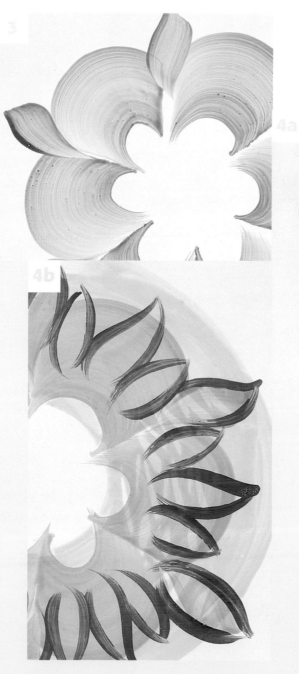

vibrant leaf and petal design

Add another layer of color to the original design and bring your pattern to another level.

YOU WILL NEED

#6 Angle Chisel Color Shaper

#6 Cup Round Color Shaper

#12 flat shader brush

#4 script liner brush

#1 script liner brush

1" (3 cm) soft wash brush

glass paint: white, turquoise, yellow, magenta, orange

step one Complete the original pattern. With a wash brush, apply a layer of orange over the prepared pattern. Using the #6 Cup Round Color Shaper, form a series of petal strokes through the wet paint, by pushing down and away with the tip of the shaper. A new design is formed. Follow final baking instructions.

magenta and purple leaf design

Try combining different techniques to create unique effects.

YOU WILL NEED

3" (77 mm) Curve Wide Color Shaper, cut and notched (see diagram, p. 18)

#6 Angle Chisel Color Shaper

1" (3 cm) soft wash brush

glass paint: magenta, white, pruple

step one   With a wash brush, apply a layer of pink (magenta mixed with white) to form a border. Using the 3" (77 mm) Curve Wide Color Shaper, cut and notched, form a wavy stripe through the wet paint. Dry and set (see p. 7).

step two   With the wash brush, apply a layer of purple paint over prepared background. Using the #6 Angle Chisel Color Shaper, form a series of leaf strokes through the wet paint to form a fern motif. Follow final baking instructions.

Deep glass bowl

1-1/2" (38 mm) Curve Wide Color Shaper, cut and notched (see diagram)

#6 Flat Chisel Color Shaper

1" (3 cm) soft wash brush

millefiori bowl

In traditional millefiori, canes of glass are sliced to create a mosaiclike effect. This technique dates back to Roman times and is used in Venetian glass. The definition of millefiori is a "thousand flowers" because many of the small circular shapes form intricate floral designs. Contemporary art glass uses this traditional technique to create abstract designs. The painted bowl is a contemporary interpretation of millefiori where simple circular shapes are repeated to form a pattern. Only the outside of the bowl is decorated, making it safe to store fruit, nuts, or candy inside.

glass paints: white, blue, citrus yellow (yellow mixed with white and a drop of green), turquoise, and magenta

▶ Wet paint is cleanly subtracted using the 1-1/2" (38 mm) Curve Wide Color Shaper, and the cut and notched tip forms clear stripes. The #6 Flat Chisel creates curvilinear and doughnut shapes. To vary your design, use the 3" (77 mm) Curve Wide, cut and notched, forming tight waves and looped lines. The #6 Cup Round can be used to create petal strokes.

starting out

Sketch your design on paper first to plan out the circles, lines, and shapes. A random, tossed pattern works well for this design. Try grouping sets of circles with some overlap.

step one   With a 1" (3 cm) wash brush, paint broad vertical stripes in white around the outside of the bowl. Dry and set (see p. 7).

step two A   With a wash brush, paint broad vertical stripes over prepared background in light blue (blue mixed with white), spaced out evenly. Using the 1-1/2" (38 mm) Curve Wide Color Shaper, cut and notched, form a vertical zigzag pattern through the wet paint. Dry and set.

step two B   With the wash brush, paint vertical stripes in yellow over prepared background. Using the 1-1/2" (38 mm) Curve Wide Color Shaper, cut and notched, make a horizontal striped pattern. Dry and set.

step three With the wash brush, apply magenta paint over the prepared background in sections. Using the #6 Flat Chisel Color Shaper, make doughnut shapes through the wet paint, representing canes of glass. Cover entire bowl with a random selection of doughnut shapes. Dry and set.

step four With a wash brush, apply a layer of turquoise paint over patterned background in sections. Using the #6 Flat Chisel Color Shaper, form additional doughnut shapes through the wet paint. The overlay of colors and shapes results in an intricate design. The play of light, color, and transparency contributes to unusual effects. Follow final baking instructions.

tip Use firm pressure when forming the doughnut shapes; wipe the tip of your shaper as you go along.

variations

orange and yellow cascading flowers

Explore other forms of millefiori designs. Here is an example of a flower pattern inspired by a traditional Italian paperweight.

YOU WILL NEED

3" (77 mm) Curve Wide Color Shaper, cut and notched (see diagram, p. 18)

#6 Flat Chisel Color Shaper

#6 Cup Round Color Shaper

1" (3 cm) soft wash brush

glass paint: magenta, white, orange, yellow

step one   With a wash brush, apply a layer of pink paint (magenta mixed with white) over the glass surface. Using a 3" (77 mm) Curve Wide Color Shaper, cut and notched, form a tight wavy pattern through the wet paint. Dry and set (see p. 7).

step two   With a wash brush, apply a layer of light yellow-orange over prepared background in sections. Using the #6 Flat Chisel Color Shaper, make doughnuts in the wet paint. Dry and set.

step 3   With a wash brush, apply a layer of orange paint over the prepared background in sections. Using the #6 Cup Round Color Shaper, form a series of petal strokes around each doughnut shape. Create a clean petal stroke by pushing down and away. Follow final baking instructions.

green and blue swirls and loops

This pattern features a series of looped lines with an overlay of c-strokes.

YOU WILL NEED

3" (77 mm) Curve Wide Color Shaper, cut and notched (see diagram, p. 18)

#6 Flat Chisel Color Shaper

1" (3 cm) soft wash brush

glass paint: yellow, green

step one With a wash brush, apply a layer of citrus yellow. Using the 3" (77 mm) Curve Wide Color Shaper, cut and notched, form a series of looped lines through the wet paint.
Dry and set (see p. 7).

step two With a wash brush, apply a layer of green over the prepared background. Using the #6 Flat Chisel Color Shaper form a cluster of c-strokes through the wet paint. Create an all over pattern. This design stretches millefiori interpretation a bit further. Follow final baking instructions.

gallery

This section features objects that combine color shaping techniques with a stretch of the imagination to form a series of functional glass art. These pieces show how the application of found glass beads and accessories can enhance an object, lending it sculptural qualities.

the author

Paula DeSimone is recognized for her accomplishments in the decorative-arts movement. She is director of the Decorative Painting Certificate Program at Rhode Island School of Design, Continuing Education, in Providence and also teaches courses in decorative arts at the Museum of Fine Arts, Boston, the Fuller Museum of Art, and the DeCordova Museum, all in Massachusetts.

Ms. DeSimone is author of *The Decorative Painter's Color Shaper Book, Painting Faux Finishes,* and is coauthor with Pat Stewart of *Brush, Sponge, Stamp,* all from Rockport Publishers. She is also featured in her own series of instructional videos, entitled *The Decorative Painter,* produced by Perspective Communications Group, Inc., of Rhode Island. You can visit her Web site at www.thedecorativepainter.com.

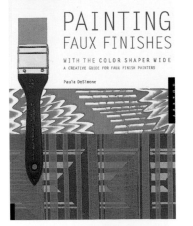

acknowledgments

I would like to extend my appreciation to Forsline and Starr International Ltd., with a very special thanks to Ladd Forsline for developing artistic tools that have inspired me to push the boundaries of creative thinking. I would also like to thank Pēbēo for their excellent glass paint, and a special thank you to Angela Scherz. My thanks to Loew-Cornell for their fine brushes. To the Rockport team and editorial staff, I express my gratitude for their continued support.

This book is dedicated to my family and friends whose love and support have enriched my life.